Dan Coates
Complete Advanced
Piano Solos

Music For All Occasions

Alfred Music
P.O. Box 10003
Van Nuys, CA 91410-0003
alfred.com

ISBN-10: 0-7692-9264-X
ISBN-13: 978-0-7692-9264-9

Contents

Dan Coates

One of today's foremost personalities in the field of printed music, Dan Coates has been providing teachers and professional musicians with quality piano material since 1975. Equally adept in arranging for beginners or accomplished musicians, his Big Note, Easy Piano and Professional Touch arrangements have made a significant contribution to the industry.

Born in Syracuse, New York, Dan began to play piano at the age of four. By the time he was 15, he'd won a New York State competition for music composers. After high school graduation, he toured the United States, Canada and Europe as an arranger and pianist with the world-famous group Up With People.

Dan settled in Miami, Florida, where he studied piano with Ivan Davis at the University of Miami while playing professionally throughout southern Florida. To date, his performance credits include appearances on "Murphy Brown" and "My Sister Sam" and at the Opening Ceremonies of the 1984 Summer Olympics in Los Angeles. Dan has also accompanied such artists as Dusty Springfield and Charlotte Rae.

In 1982, Dan began his association with Warner Bros. Publications—an association that has produced more than four hundred Dan Coates books and sheets. Throughout the year, he conducts piano workshops nationwide, during which he demonstrates his popular arrangements.

ANGEL EYES

Composed by
JIM BRICKMAN

Based on a Theme from the Warner Bros. TV Movie "THE THORN BIRDS"

ANYWHERE THE HEART GOES
(Meggie's Theme)

Words by
WILL JENNINGS

Music by
HENRY MANCINI

Anywhere the Heart Goes - 3 - 1

12

From the Emmy Award Winning TV presentation "ANNE OF GREEN GABLES"

ANNE'S THEME

Composed by
HAGWOOD HARDY

Anne's Theme - 3 - 1

14

Anne's Theme - 3 - 3

From ''ARTHUR,'' an Orion Pictures Release through WARNER BROS.

ARTHUR'S THEME
(Best That You Can Do)

Words and Music by
**BURT BACHARACH, CAROLE BAYER SAGER,
CHRISTOPHER CROSS and PETER ALLEN**

Arthur's Theme - 3 - 1

From the Warner Bros. Motion Picture "CASABLANCA"

AS TIME GOES BY

Words and Music by
HERMAN HUPFELD

Moderately, with expresssion

As Time Goes By - 3 - 1

As Time Goes By - 3 - 3

From the Soundtrack of the PBS Series "THE CIVIL WAR," a Film by Ken Burns

ASHOKAN FAREWELL

By
JAY UNGAR

Ashokan Farewell - 3 - 1

From Walt Disney's "BEAUTY AND THE BEAST"

BEAUTY AND THE BEAST

Lyrics by
HOWARD ASHMAN

Music by
ALAN MENKEN

Beauty and the Beast - 5 - 1

BECAUSE YOU LOVED ME
(Theme from "UP CLOSE & PERSONAL")

Words and Music by
DIANE WARREN

Because You Loved Me - 4 - 1

Because You Loved Me - 4 - 2

From the WARNER BROS. Film "SUPERMAN"

CAN YOU READ MY MIND?

Love Theme from "Superman"

Words by
LESLIE BRICUSSE

Music by
JOHN WILLIAMS

Can You Read My Mind? - 4 - 1

Can You Read My Mind? - 4 - 2

Can You Read My Mind? - 4 - 4

CANON IN D
(Pachelbel)

JOHANN PACHELBEL
(1653-1706)

Canon in D - 4 - 1

Canon in D - 4 - 2

From the Broadway Musical Production "BARNUM"

THE COLORS OF MY LIFE

Music by
CY COLEMAN

Lyrics by
MICHAEL STEWART

The Colors of My Life - 4 - 1

44

The Colors of My Life - 4 - 3

The Colors of My Life - 4 - 4

From Walt Disney's "POCAHONTAS"

COLORS OF THE WIND

Lyrics by
STEPHEN SCHWARTZ

Music by
ALAN MENKEN

Colors of the Wind - 5 - 3

cresc. poco a poco

rall.

ff meno mosso

decresc.

FROM A DISTANCE

Lyrics and Music by
JULIE GOLD

54

DESPERADO

Words and Music by
DON HENLEY and GLENN FREY

Desperado - 4 - 1

From Walt Disney's "CINDERELLA"

A DREAM IS A WISH YOUR HEART MAKES

Words and Music by
MACK DAVID, AL HOFFMAN
and JERRY LIVINGSTON

Slowly, with expression

A Dream Is a Wish Your Heart Makes - 4 - 3

A Dream Is a Wish Your Heart Makes - 4 - 4

From "A STAR IS BORN"

EVERGREEN

Words by
PAUL WILLIAMS

Music by
BARBRA STREISAND

Moderately slow, flowing

Evergreen - 6 - 1

Evergreen - 6 - 4

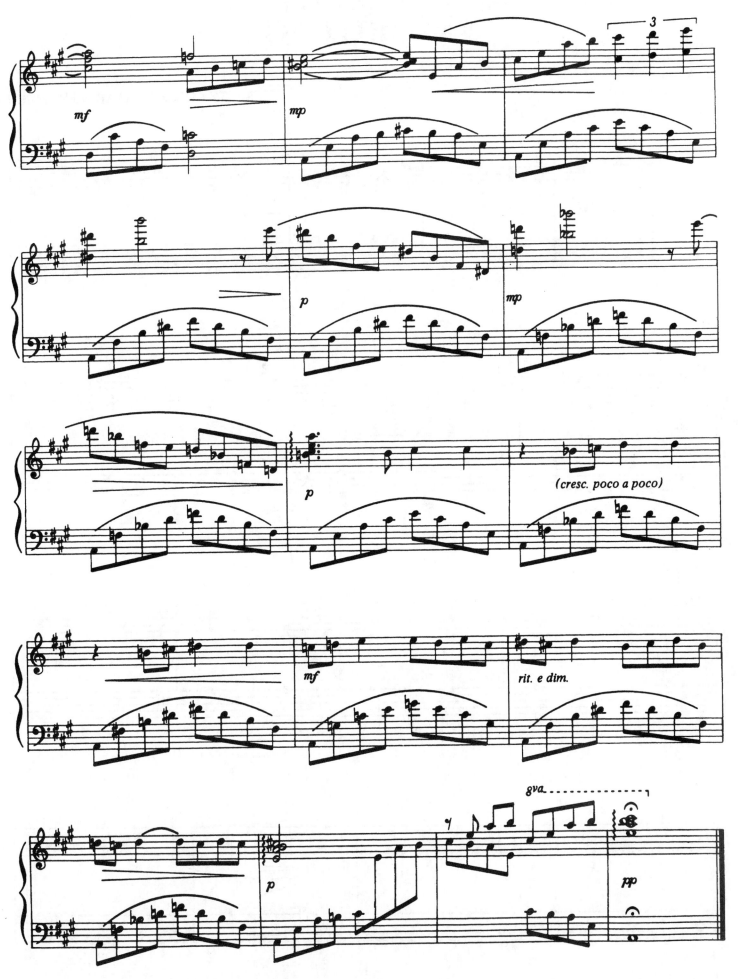

From the Musical "THE WILL ROGERS FOLLIES"

FAVORITE SON

Music by
CY COLEMAN

Lyrics by
BETTY COMDEN and ADOLPH GREEN

Lively 2 ♩ = 120

Favorite Son - 4 - 1

FOREVER

Words by
KENNY LOGGINS and
EVA EIN LOGGINS

Music by
KENNY LOGGINS and
DAVID FOSTER

Moderately Slow

Forever - 6 - 1

Forever - 6 - 4

Coda

FRIENDS AND LOVERS
(Both to Each Other)

Words and Music by
PAUL GORDON and JAY GRUSKA

Friends and Lovers - 4 - 1

Friends and Lovers - 4 - 2

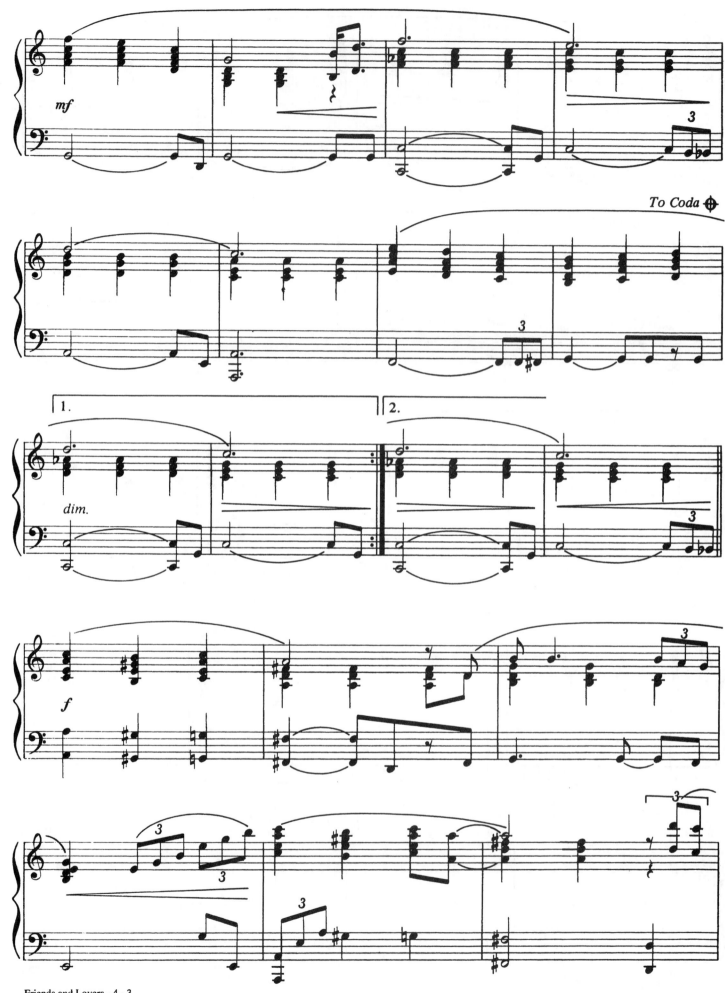

To Coda ⊕

Friends and Lovers - 4 - 3

D.S. 𝄋 al Coda ⊕

Coda

From the Columbia Picture "THE GREATEST" - A Columbia/EMI Presentation

THE GREATEST LOVE OF ALL

By
LINDA CREED and
MICHAEL MASSER

The Greatest Love of All - 5 - 1

The Greatest Love of All - 5 - 4

88

The Greatest Love of All - 5 - 5

HAPPY BIRTHDAY TO YOU!

Words and Music by
MILDRED J. HILL and PATTY S. HILL

(*Insert name of celebrant)

From the Broadway Musical Production "DAMN YANKEES"

HEART

Words and Music by
RICHARD ADLER and JERRY ROSS

Heart - 4 - 1

From the Musical "THE PAJAMA GAME"

HEY THERE

Words and Music by
RICHARD ADLER and JERRY ROSS

Moderately slow "swing" feel ♩ = 76

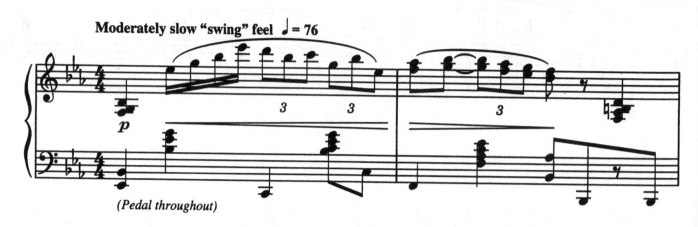

(Pedal throughout)

Hey There - 4 - 1

THE HOMECOMING

By
HAGOOD HARDY

Moderately slow, with expression

The Homecoming - 4 - 1

The Homecoming - 4 - 2

The Homecoming - 4 - 4

From "THE SECRET GARDEN"

HOW COULD I EVER KNOW?

Lyrics by
MARSHA NORMAN

Music by
LUCY SIMON

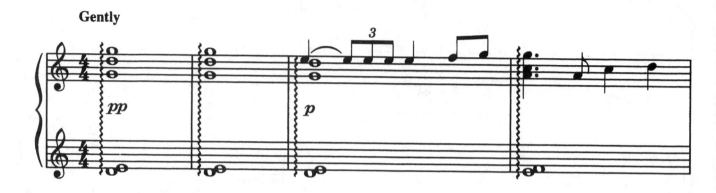

How Could I Ever Know? - 4 - 1

Meno mosso

HOW DO I LIVE

Words and Music by
DIANE WARREN

Moderately slow ♩ = 92

(with pedal)

How Do I Live - 4 - 1

How Do I Live - 4 - 2

How Do I Live - 4 - 4

I BELIEVE I CAN FLY

Words and Music by
R. KELLY

I Believe I Can Fly - 4 - 1

I Believe I Can Fly - 4 - 2

I Believe I Can Fly - 4 - 4

From the Warner Bros. Motion Picture "BEST FRIENDS"

HOW DO YOU KEEP THE MUSIC PLAYING?

Words by
ALAN and MARILYN BERGMAN

Music by
MICHEL LEGRAND

How Do You Keep the Music Playing? - 3 - 1

How Do You Keep the Music Playing? - 3 - 2

How Do You Keep the Music Playing? - 3 - 3

(EVERYTHING I DO) I DO IT FOR YOU

Lyrics and Music by
BRYAN ADAMS, R.J. LANGE and M. KAMEN

(Everything I Do) I Do It for You - 3 - 1

(Everything I Do) I Do It for You - 3 - 2

(Everything I Do) I Do It for You - 3 - 3

I CAN LOVE YOU LIKE THAT

Wods and Music by
STEVE DIAMOND, MARIBETH DERRY
and JENNIFER KIMBALL

I Can Love You Like That - 4 - 1

122

I SAY A LITTLE PRAYER

Words by
HAL DAVID

Music by
BURT BACHARACH

I Say a Little Prayer - 4 - 1

From Touchstone Pictures' ARMAGEDDON

I DON'T WANT TO MISS A THING

Words and Music by
DIANE WARREN

I Don't Want to Miss a Thing - 5 - 1

I Don't Want to Miss a Thing - 5 - 2

I Don't Want to Miss a Thing - 5 - 3

I Don't Want to Miss a Thing - 5 - 4

IF YOU BELIEVE

Composed by
JIM BRICKMAN

If You Believe - 5 - 1

I SWEAR

Words and Music by
GARY BAKER and FRANK MYERS

I Swear - 4 - 1

I WILL ALWAYS LOVE YOU

Words and Music by
DOLLY PARTON

Slowly, with expression

From the Broadway Musical Production "SWEET CHARITY"

IF MY FRIENDS COULD SEE ME NOW!

Music by
CY COLEMAN

Lyric by
DOROTHY FIELDS

Bright strut tempo

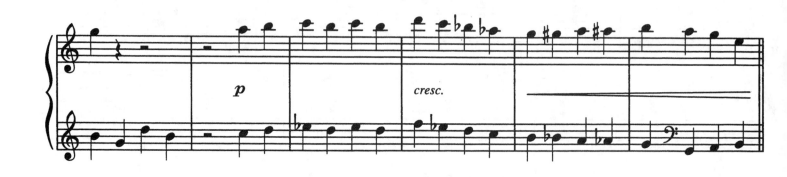

If My Friends Could See Me Now! - 4 - 1

If My Friends Could See Me Now! - 4 - 2

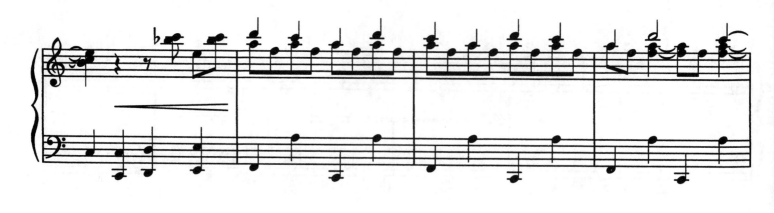

If My Friends Could See Me Now! - 4 - 4

IN THIS LIFE

Words and Music by
MIKE REID and
ALLEN SHAMBLIN

In This Life - 4 - 1

To Coda ⊕

decresc.

In This Life - 4 - 2

KAREN'S THEME

Composed by
RICHARD CARPENTER

Karen's Theme - 4 - 1

Karen's Theme - 4 - 4

KEI'S SONG

Music by
DAVID BENOIT

Kei's Song - 3 - 1

To Coda ⊕

160

Theme from the TV Series "MARRIED . . . WITH CHILDREN"

LOVE AND MARRIAGE

Words by
SAMMY CAHN

Music by
JAMES VAN HEUSEN

Love and Marriage - 3 - 1

162

Love and Marriage - 3 - 2

Love and Marriage - 3 - 3

LOVE SOLO

Music by
DAN COATES

Moderately slow, with expression

Love Solo - 3 - 1

From the Motion Picture "M*A*S*H"

SONG FROM M*A*S*H
(Suicide Is Painless)

Words and Music by
MIKE ALTMAN and JOHNNY MANDEL

Moderately fast

168

to Coda ⊕

D.S. ℘ al ⊕ Coda

crescendo

Song From M*A*S*H - 3 - 2

MAY YOU ALWAYS

Words and Music by
LARRY MARKES and DICK CHARLES

May You Always - 3 - 1

May You Always - 3 - 2

MISTY

Words by
JOHNNY BURKE

Music by
ERROLL GARNER

Misty - 3 - 3

From the Movie "THE COLOR PURPLE," a Stephen Spielberg Film
Nominee, Best Original Song, 1985

MISS CELIE'S BLUES
(Sister)

Words by
QUINCY JONES, ROD TEMPERTON
and LIONEL RICHIE

Music by
QUINCY JONES and ROD TEMPERTON

Miss Celie's Blues - 4 - 1

Miss Celie's Blues - 4 - 2

From the Musical Production "THE WILL ROGERS FOLLIES"

MY UNKNOWN SOMEONE

Music by
CY COLEMAN

Lyrics by
BETTY COMDEN and ADOLPH GREEN

My Unknown Someone - 4 - 1

Moderately, with feeling

MY ONE TRUE FRIEND
(From ''ONE TRUE THING'')

Words and Music by
CAROLE BAYER SAGER, CAROLE KING
and DAVID FOSTER

My One True Friend - 5 - 1

My One True Friend - 5 - 4

From the Twentieth Century-Fox Film "THE OTHER SIDE OF MIDNIGHT"

NOELLE'S THEME
(The Other Side Of Midnight)

Music by
MICHEL LEGRAND

Noelle's Theme - 3 - 1

Noelle's Theme - 3 - 2

Noelle's Theme - 3 - 3

OH! WHAT IT SEEMED TO BE

Words and Music by
BENNIE BENJAMIN,
GEORGE DAVID WEISS and FRANKIE CARLE

Oh! What It Seemed to Be - 3 - 1

194

Oh! What It Seemed to Be - 3 - 3

ONCE BEFORE I GO

Words and Music by
PETER ALLEN and DEAN PITCHFORD

Once Before I Go - 5 - 1

(a little faster)

Once Before I Go - 5 - 5

ONE MOMENT IN TIME

Words and Music by
ALBERT HAMMOND
and JOHN BETTIS

One Moment in Time - 5 - 1

One Moment in Time - 5 - 3

OPEN ARMS

Words and Music by
STEVE PERRY and JONATHAN CAIN

Open Arms - 3 - 1

From the Motion Picture "THE WIZARD OF OZ"

OVER THE RAINBOW

Lyric by
E. Y. HARBURG

Music by
HAROLD ARLEN

Slowly, with expression ♩ = 82

Over the Rainbow - 6 - 1

THE PRAYER

Words and Music by
CAROLE BAYER SAGER and DAVID FOSTER

(L.H. simile throughout)

The Prayer - 4 - 1

The Prayer - 4 - 2

RAGTIME

Music by
STEPHEN FLAHERTY

Ragtime - 6 - 1

Ragtime - 6 - 2

Ragtime - 6 - 4

Grand cakewalk

From the Twentieth Century-Fox Motion Picture "THE ROSE"

THE ROSE

Words and Music by
AMANDA McBROOM

The Rose - 3 - 1

poco rit.

a tempo

p

poco cresc. - - - - - - - - - - - -

mp

mf

8va bassa

mf

8va bassa

The Rose - 3 - 2

From the Warner Bros.-Seven Arts Film "PICASSO SUMMER"

SUMMER ME, WINTER ME
(Theme from "Picasso Summer")

Lyrics by
ALAN and MARILYN BERGMAN

Music by
MICHEL LEGRAND

Summer Me, Winter Me - 3 - 1

228

Summer Me, Winter Me - 3 - 3

SAVING ALL MY LOVE FOR YOU

Words by
GERRY GOFFIN

Music by
MICHAEL MASSER

Slowly

Saving All My Love for You - 4 - 1

Saving All My Love for You - 4 - 4

From the Broadway Musical Productiion "A LITTLE NIGHT MUSIC"

SEND IN THE CLOWNS

Music and Lyrics by
STEPHEN SONDHEIM

Send in the Clowns - 4 - 1

Columbia Pictures Presents A New Vision Production "WHITE NIGHTS"

SEPARATE LIVES
(Love Theme from "White Nights")

Words and Music by
STEPHEN BISHOP

Freely, with expression

Separate Lives - 4 - 1

Slowly, with expression

240

From the Broadway Musical "SHE LOVES ME"

SHE LOVES ME

Lyrics by
SHELDON HARNICK

Music by
JERRY BOCK

She Loves Me - 4 - 1

From the Twentieth Century-Fox Motion Picture "STAR WARS"

STAR WARS
(Main Theme)

Music by
JOHN WILLIAMS

Star Wars - 2 - 1

TEARS IN HEAVEN

Words and Music by
WILL JENNINGS and ERIC CLAPTON

Tears in Heaven - 4 - 1

Tears in Heaven - 4 - 2

TELL HIM

Words and Music by
LINDA THOMPSON, DAVID FOSTER
and WALTER AFANASIEFF

Tell Him - 6 - 1

cresc. poco a poco

f

Tell Him - 6 - 4

From the Columbia Motion Picture "ICE CASTLES"

THEME FROM ICE CASTLES
(Through the Eyes of Love)

Lyrics by
CAROLE BAYER SAGER

Music by
MARVIN HAMLISCH

Slowly, with feeling

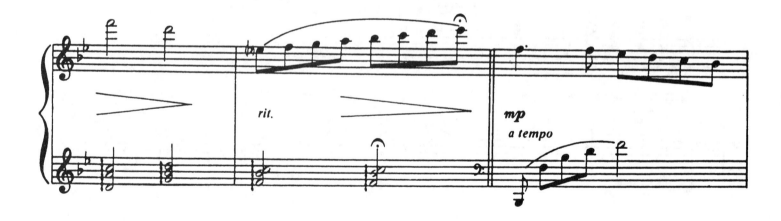

Theme from Ice Castles - 4 - 1

Theme from Ice Castles - 4 - 3

Theme from Ice Castles - 4 - 4

THAT'S WHAT FRIENDS ARE FOR

Words and Music by
CAROLE BAYER SAGER and BURT BACHARACH

That's What Friends Are For - 3 - 1

To Coda ⊕

From the United Artists Motion Picture "NEW YORK, NEW YORK"

THEME FROM NEW YORK, NEW YORK

Words by
FRED EBB

Music by
JOHN KANDER

Moderately, with rhythm

Theme from New York, New York - 5 - 1

Theme from New York, New York - 5 - 5

TIME TO SAY GOODBYE
(Con Te Partiró)

Lyrics by LUCIO QUARANTOTTO
English Lyrics by FRANK PETERSON

Music by
FRANCESCO SARORI

TONIGHT I CELEBRATE MY LOVE

Words and Music by
MICHAEL MASSER and GERRY GOFFIN

Moderately Slow (♩ = 60)

Tonight I Celebrate My Love - 3 - 1

UN-BREAK MY HEART

Words and Music by
DIANE WARREN

Un-Break My Heart - 4 - 1

VALENTINE

Composed by
JIM BRICKMAN and JACK KUGELL

Moderately slow (♩ = 92)

Valentine - 4 - 1

From the Motion Picture "AN OFFICER AND A GENTLEMAN"

UP WHERE WE BELONG

Words by
WILL JENNINGS

Music by
JACK NITZSCHE and BUFFY SAINTE-MARIE

Up Where We Belong - 3 - 1

WE'VE GOT TONIGHT

Words and Music by
BOB SEGER

We've Got Tonight - 5 - 1

We've Got Tonight - 5 - 3

We've Got Tonight - 5 - 5

WHAT'S NEW?

Words by
JOHNNY BURKE

Music by
BOB HAGGART

What's New? - 2 - 1

From the Musical Production "CITY OF ANGELS"

YOU CAN ALWAYS COUNT ON ME

Music by
CY COLEMAN

Lyrics by
DAVID ZIPPEL

You Can Always Count on Me - 4 - 1

𝄋 **Moderately (Swing feel)**

To Coda ⊕

You Can Always Count on Me - 4 - 4

LA VIE EN ROSE
(La-Vee-On Rose)

Original French Words by
EDITH PIAF
English Words by
MACK DAVID

Music by
LOUIGUY

Slowly, with expression

La Vie En Rose - 2 - 1

La Vie En Rose - 2 - 2

From the Original Motion Picture Soundtrack "BEACHES"

THE WIND BENEATH MY WINGS

Words and Music by
LARRY HENLEY and JEFF SILBAR

The Wind Beneath My Wings - 3 - 1